You can Save the Planet

Something Old, Something New: Recycling

Anita Ganeri

Heinemann Library
Chicago, Illinois

Customer Service 888-454-2279
Visit our website at www.heinemannlibrary.com

Designed by Richard Parker and Q2A Solutions
Photo research by Maria Joannou and Virginia Stroud-Lewis
Printed in China by WKT Company Limited

09 08 07
10 9 8 7 6 5 4 3 2

Library of Congress Cataloging-in-Publication Data
Ganeri, Anita, 1961-
    Something old, something new : recycling / Anita Ganeri.-- 1st ed.
        p. cm. -- (You can save the planet)
Includes bibliographical references and index.
ISBN 1-4034-6843-5 (hc, library binding) -- ISBN 1-4034-6849-4 (pb)
ISBN 978-1-4034-6843-7 (HC)   ISBN 978-1-4034-6849-9 (pbk)
1. Recycling (Waste, etc.)--Juvenile literature. 2. Waste
minimization--Juvenile literature. I. Title. II. Series.
    TD794.5.G36 2005
    363.72'82--dc22
                                    2004020590

Acknowledgments
The author and publishers are grateful to the following for permission to reproduce copyright material:
pp. 4, 7, 10, 11, 17, 18, 19, 21, 22, 25 Tudor Photography; p. 5 Mark Boulton/ICCE; p. 8 Simon Fraser/Northumbrian
Environmental, Management Ltd./Science Photo Library; pp. 9, 14, 16 Alamy; p. 12 Lester Lefkowitz/Corbis; p. 13 Image
Bank/Getty Images; p. 15 Jean Heguy/Corbis; p. 20 Michael S. Yamashita/Corbis; p. 23 Tim Dirven/Panos Pictures; p. 24
Ecoscene; p. 26 Chris Sattlberger/Panos Pictures; p. 27 Dorothy Burrows/Photofusion.

Cover photograph by Ecoscene/Angela Hampton.

Contents

Some words are shown in bold, **like this**. You can find out what they mean by looking in the glossary.

What Is Waste?

Waste is anything we throw away. We throw away some things, such as drink cans and newspapers, because we do not need them anymore. We throw away other things, such as toys and refrigerators, when they are broken or worn out.

What is the problem?

Waste is a big problem for our planet. We have to find places to put all the waste we throw away, and we are running out of space. Besides, every time we throw something away, we waste precious materials. Waste is bad for the **environment**. It can harm and kill plants and animals, including humans.

Every time you throw away something, you are wasting the material in it and the energy used to make it.

4

The three Rs

We need to find ways to throw less waste away. There are three ways to do this. These are known as the three Rs. The first R is for reduce, which means cutting down on the things we buy so that we have to throw less away. The second R is for reuse, which means using old things again instead of throwing them away. The third R is for recycle, which means making new things out of old. Things should only be thrown away when we cannot reuse or recycle them.

These are shoes made from reused car tires.

Taking Action: What Can I Do?

If we keep throwing away so much waste, we are storing up problems for people in the future. You might think that the problem of waste is too big for you to do anything about. But if each of us makes a small effort, together we can make a big difference. Look for Taking Action boxes like this one throughout this book. They will give you ideas for things you can do to reduce, reuse, and recycle.

What do we throw away?

Think about all the garbage you made today. You might be surprised. Among the things you might have thrown away are cereal boxes, plastic milk bottles, used writing paper, drink cans, snack wrappers, and apple cores. But you are not alone. The rest of your family produces garbage, too. So does every other family, office, store, school, and factory in your community and country. That is an enormous amount of waste.

How much waste?

In **developed** countries, such as the United States, Great Britain, and Australia, each household throws away about 2,200 pounds (1,000 kilograms) of waste every year. Each year we throw away more waste than the year before. In most developed countries, only about a tenth of this waste is reused or recycled. This chart shows how much and what sort of waste a typical household in a developed country throws away.

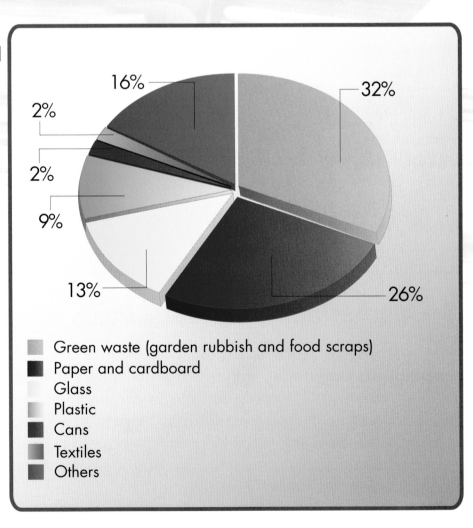

16% 2% 2% 9% 13% 32% 26%

- Green waste (garden rubbish and food scraps)
- Paper and cardboard
- Glass
- Plastic
- Cans
- Textiles
- Others

Every day we throw away
many types of materials.
Some could be recycled.

Wasted energy

It takes lots of energy to make brand-new things. For example, the energy used to make an aluminum drink can in a factory would power a television for three hours. When we throw something away, we are also throwing away the energy used to make it. Energy is precious. Most of it comes from burning **fossil fuels**, which harms the environment.

Taking Action: A Waste Diary

Try keeping a waste diary for a week at home or school. Ask a parent or teacher to help. At the end of each day, empty all the wastebaskets and garbage cans at home or in your classroom into one bag and weigh it. Draw a chart that shows the weight of waste you collect each day. Add up the weekly waste total.

Where Does our Waste Go?

Waste is collected from your home or school by garbage trucks. Machinery in the trucks crushes the waste so that it takes up less space. The trucks unload the waste at a **waste transfer station**. Some waste is taken away to be recycled. Some waste is burned. The rest is taken to **landfill** sites.

Dozens of trucks dump their loads of garbage into a landfill site every day.

What happens at a landfill site?

At a landfill site, waste is tipped into a huge hole. The hole is lined with plastic and clay to keep liquid from the waste from leaking out. When the site is full, the waste is covered with a layer of soil. But we should not forget about the buried waste. Dangerous liquids and gases can come from the site, and some of the waste will take thousands of years to **rot** away. Landfill sites also look ugly and smell bad. After a few years, parks or golf courses can be built on the site. But it is hard to build houses because the ground sinks as the waste rots.

Some waste is burned in incinerators. The ash from the waste is then buried in the ground.

Science Behind It: Liquid and Gas

Some waste rots away naturally in landfill sites, just as dead plants rot away in the garden. But as the waste rots, it makes **methane** gas, which is explosive. Rotting also makes a black liquid called leachate, which can contain dangerous chemicals. Both the methane and leachate can be dangerous if they leak into the ground around the site. They must be collected for many years after the site is full.

What Are the Three Rs?

What is reducing?

Reducing is the first of the three Rs. It means not buying things that will be thrown away soon after buying them. Reducing is the best way to cut down on waste. Next time you go shopping, think about how you can reduce the amount you buy and, in turn, reduce the amount you waste.

Taking Action

Here are some ideas for reducing waste:

- Try not to buy things with lots of **packaging**. You will just throw it away when you get home. For example, buy loose apples instead of apples packed on a tray and covered with plastic.
- Take your lunch and snacks to school in reusable plastic containers instead of wrapping them in foil or plastic food wrap.
- Reuse scraps of colored paper and fabric as art materials at school.
- Don't buy **disposable** things. If you are going on a picnic, don't buy paper plates and plastic knifes and forks which you will later throw away. Take washable, reusable plastic plates and metal silverware instead.
- Buy good quality things that will last a long time.
- Use **rechargeable batteries** instead of disposable batteries.

Some things we buy have more packaging than they need. How much waste does this create?

What is reusing?

Reusing is the second of the three Rs. Reusing means using things again, instead of throwing them away. Some things can be used again in the same way. For example, you can reuse envelopes several times before they are worn out. You can also reuse things in a new way. For example, you could use an old plastic margarine tub for storing paper clips.

Neaten up your desk with reused food containers.

Taking Action: Sell and Donate

Try not to throw anything away that somebody else could use. You may have old toys and games, videos, books, or clothes that you no longer use. Get permission to collect them and organize a sale with your friends. You could hold the sale at school or in a garage or yard. You could also give the things to a local resale shop.

What is recycling?

Recycling is the third of the three Rs. Recycling means using the materials in old objects to make new objects. For example, the glass in old bottles can be recycled to make new bottles. The aluminum in old drink cans can be used to make new cans. Some materials can be recycled hundreds of times.

These trees have been cut down to make things for people to use, such as paper.

Why should we recycle?

There are two main reasons for recycling. It saves the precious **natural resources** needed to make new materials. For example, when you recycle paper, fewer trees need to be cut down to make new paper. When you recycle plastic, oil and natural gas supplies do not have to be used to make new plastic. Recycling also saves energy and other resources such as water and chemicals. Recycling is not always the best thing to do. Some materials use more energy to recycle than to make new.

What can we recycle?

Hundreds of different things can be recycled, from plastic bottles to whole cars. It is easiest to recycle things that are made of just one material, such as newspapers, glass bottles, or aluminum cans. These things are broken down or melted. More complicated things, such as computers and refrigerators, have to be taken apart to separate out the different materials.

Science Behind It: Does Recycling Save Energy?

Making anything uses energy. Think of a soup can made of steel. It took energy to mine the rock that the iron came from. Then, the rock has to be transported to the factory where the iron is taken out of the rock, made into steel, and made into the can. By recycling the can, almost all of that energy can be saved.

The materials used to make steel cans must be heated to a very high temperature. This uses lots of energy.

collecting for recycling

In many communities, people place their recycling bins on the curb once a week. City workers then take them to be recycled. If your community does not have curbside recycling, you can take your recyclables to a local recycling center. Local recycling centers may also recycle items you cannot put in your bins such as motor oil, car batteries, and paint.

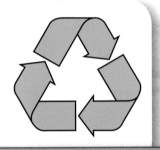

This logo tells you that something can be recycled, or that it is made from recycled materials.

Always sort waste properly before putting it into recycling bins.

Taking your waste for recycling is a very good idea. But do not make a special trip in a car to your recycling center if you have only got one or two bottles or newspapers to throw away. The **pollution** from the car and the energy used up would cancel out all the good you would be doing by recycling!

Taking Action: Buy Recycled

Companies will not make products from recycled materials if people do not buy them. So the best way to encourage recycling is to buy recycled things when you can. Look out for the recycled logo on items such as toilet paper and paper towels. At school, find out if writing paper and toilet paper are made from recycled paper.

Can We Cut Down on Waste Paper?

Every day, we throw away millions of newspapers and magazines, huge piles of printer paper, envelopes, junk mail, and cardboard. Paper and cardboard make up about quarter of all **household waste**. Offices throw even more away. By putting the three Rs into action, you can easily cut down on how much paper you waste.

This is a large pile of old newspapers and magazines. Think of the trees that were cut down to make them!

Reducing and reusing paper

There are lots of ways of cutting down on the amount of paper and cardboard you use at school and at home. Here are some ideas:

- Always write on both sides of a sheet of paper.
- Don't start a new page in a notebook until the last page is finished.
- Only print out what you really need when using a computer.
- Share newspapers and magazines with your friends instead of buying one each.
- Reuse cardboard boxes for storage.
- Ask your family to cancel junk mail, if they can.

15

Taking Action: Paper Recycling

Paper is one of the easiest materials to recycle. You can buy recycled writing paper and wrapping paper. Many newspapers are printed on recycled paper. At home, make sure newspapers, magazines, and other types of paper are recycled if possible. Do you have a paper recycling program at school? If not, ask your teachers if you can start one. Put waste paper in a separate bin. Advertise the program by putting up posters and announcing it on your school website or in your school newspaper.

A few seconds spent recycling can save a lot of energy and a lot of trees!

Science Behind It: New and Recycled Paper

Paper is made from tiny **fibers** glued together. Most of the fibers come from conifer trees that have been specially grown for making paper. The wood is mashed and broken up to get the fibers out. Turning trees into paper uses lots of energy, water, and other chemicals. Recycling paper saves trees and energy.

case Study: Paper for Worms

When the children at Mildura West Primary School in Australia looked into recycling, they found that some types of paper, such as envelopes and used photocopier paper, could not be recycled in their area. Instead, it went into **landfill** sites. The children discovered a clever way of reusing the paper. Worms can eat shredded paper, so the children decided to shred their waste paper and send it to local worm farms, where worms are raised for fishers to use as bait.

The children put up posters to advertise their program to people in their community and invited experts to talk to students and parents. They told people in their community how to collect and shred waste paper and set up a service to collect the paper from people's homes. The school was given money to buy two paper-shredding machines. In 2003, the school won a Waste Wise award for their work.

One good way to reuse paper is to feed it to worms. The worms can then be sold.

Can We Recycle old cans?

The answer is: yes, we can! Most drink cans are made from aluminum. Most food cans are made from steel. You can recycle both of these metals. Collect your cans in a box. Ask an adult to help you find out where you can take cans to be recycled. As well as saving **natural resources**, you will also be saving energy. It takes twenty times more energy to make a new aluminum drink can than to make one from recycled metal.

What about other metal things?

Most metal things can be recycled. Like drink cans, kitchen foil, and foil food dishes are made from aluminum. These items as well as larger metal objects, such as old bicycle frames, may be recyclable. Ask your community's recycling center if you can recycle them.

If a magnet sticks to the can, it is probably made of steel. If it does not stick, it is probably made of aluminum. Steel and aluminum cans are often recycled separately.

Science Behind It: Metals from Rocks

Metals such as aluminum are **extracted** from rocks called ores. First, the ore is dug from the ground and crushed. Then, it is heated in a container until it melts. This releases the aluminum. Electricity is passed through the molten (melted) ore, which makes the aluminum flow out. The aluminum cools and turns to solid metal. All this uses a lot of energy, which is why it is better to recycle metals.

Can We Use Glass Again?

Glass makes up about five to ten percent of **household waste**. Families in **developed** countries throw away as many as 500 glass jars and bottles every year. Unfortunately, glass does not **rot** away. It lasts for thousands of years in a **landfill** site. All of this waste glass could be reused or recycled.

How can we reuse glass?

You can use some glass bottles and jars again and again. For example, empty glass jars can be used as vases for flowers or for storing small objects such as pens and paper clips. You can also mix and store paint in glass jars. Sometimes glass is crushed into small chunks and mixed to make road surfaces.

You can reuse glass jars by keeping things in them instead of throwing them away.

Science Behind It: Recycling Bottles

Glass is made from sand, a material called soda ash, and limestone. These ingredients are melted together and poured into molds to make bottles. When people recycle glass, new **raw materials** do not have to be used. Glass bottles are easy to recycle. They are crushed to make a material called cullet, which is melted down and then used to make new bottles.

This shows uncrushed glass bottles on the right and crushed glass cullet on the left at a a recycling center.

Taking Action: Sorting Glass

Glass comes in different colors. The main colors are clear, brown, and green. If these colors are mixed when they are recycled, the new glass comes out looking muddy. Glass bottles and jars must be sorted by color, either by you or by workers at the recycling center. Check with your recycling center to find out if you need to sort your glass or if they will do it. Remember to wear gloves when you handle or sort glass as it may be broken.

What Can We Do with old Plastic?

Plastic is a very useful material. It can be molded into almost any shape. We use it to make thousands of objects, from tiny toys to patio furniture. Every year, we throw away millions of plastic bags, bottles, and containers. Unfortunately, plastic does not **rot** away. It lasts for hundreds of years. Plastic is made from oil (petroleum) and natural gas. Wasting plastic also wastes these precious supplies. Oil and natural gas supplies will not last forever, and when they run out there will be no more.

Many of the things we buy and use every day are packaged in plastic. Most of the plastic gets thrown away, but some could be recycled.

The simplest way to cut down on the amount of plastic we throw away is to reduce the plastic **packaging** we buy. You can help by not buying things that have lots of plastic packaging. You can also reuse plastic containers. For example, yogurt and cottage-cheese cartons make excellent storage containers, and you can refill plastic bottles with drinks to take to school.

Can plastic be recycled?

There are more than 50 different types of plastic. Some plastics cannot be recycled. Some can be recycled but cannot be mixed together. This means we have to sort plastics carefully before they can be recycled. Plastics that can be recycled usually have a symbol on them. Check with your recycling center to find out which types of plastic can be recycled in your area. Always wash out plastic bottles and containers before you recycle them.

Recycled plastics are used to make hundreds of different objects, such as garbage bags, grocery bags, and other packaging as well as plumbing pipes. Some fleece jackets are made from recycled drink bottles.

Carefully check the symbols on your plastic bottles, to see which types of plastic they are.

Taking Action: Plastic Bags for Life

In Britain, people throw away about eight billion plastic bags every year! You can easily reuse plastic bags by taking them back to the supermarket the next time you visit. Or you can use them for kitchen waste instead of buying garbage bags. Better still, buy a cloth shopping bag that will last for hundreds of shopping trips.

Case Study: Reusing Eyeglasses

Most eyeglasses lenses are made from plastic. They are expensive to make because the plastic must be very pure and the lenses must be made very accurately. They cannot be made from recycled plastic. Glasses frames are also expensive to make. Glasses are not usually recycled because they do not contain enough plastic and metal to make it worthwhile. Millions of pairs of glasses are thrown away every year. However, a charity called Vision Aid Overseas has found a way to reuse glasses and to help poor people at the same time.

How are glasses reused?

In many countries, people with poor eyesight cannot afford glasses, and life is difficult for them. Vision Aid Overseas collects old glasses in Britain. Then **opticians** take them to poorer countries such as Kenya and India. The opticians test people's eyesight and give them the right glasses to wear.

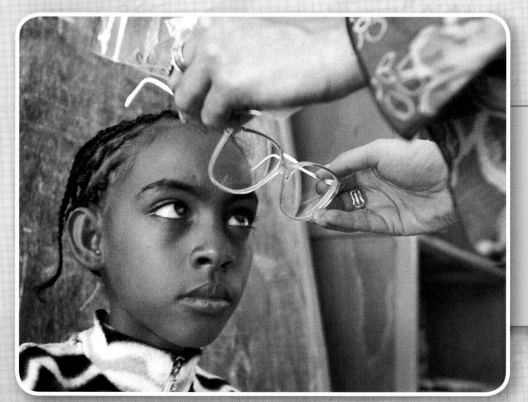

This girl will be able to see better with the reused glasses she is being given.

Can We Recycle Plants?

About a quarter of **household waste** is plant waste, or "green waste," from kitchens and gardens. It is mostly made of fruit and vegetable peelings, grass clippings, and weeds. Green waste **rots** naturally, but it causes problems when it is buried in **landfill** sites. It takes up lots of space, and it produces **methane** gas. But you can easily recycle green waste at school and at home to make **compost**.

Can we use methane?

Methane can be useful. At some landfill sites, methane is collected and sent to nearby factories, where it is burned for heating. This methane is called biogas. Plant waste can be put into special containers called digesters. Here it rots to produce methane, which can be burned for heating and cooking.

This small-scale biogas system was designed to heat the house.

Science Behind It: What Is Biodegradable?

Dead plants and animals are biodegradable. This means that they rot away naturally. They rot because **microorganisms** such as **bacteria** and **fungi** feed on them. The microorganisms turn the remains into simple chemicals that mix into the soil, where new plants use them to grow. In this way, dead plants and animals are recycled naturally. Materials such as metals, glass, and plastic are not biodegradable.

Taking Action: Making Compost

Compost is easy to make. You can buy a compost bin or make one from scrap wood. Put the bin on a patch of soil in a sunny place. Simply put green waste into the bin and mix it with a pitchfork. After about six months, the compost at the bottom of the bin will have turned dark and crumbly. Now it is ready to put on the garden. You can compost:

- vegetable and fruit peelings
- grass clippings
- hedge trimmings
- leaves
- used tea bags and coffee grounds
- shredded paper

You should not put any meat, fish scraps, or cooked food into compost. It will attract mice and other pests.

Adding a good mixture of different vegetable wastes to your compost bin makes good, rich compost.

What Else Can We Recycle?

There are not many things that cannot be reused or recycled. To reuse old clothes, sell them at a garage sale or give them to a resale shop. Furniture can also be reused. Even complicated machines can be broken up and their parts recycled. Before throwing away a broken machine or appliance, first see if it can be repaired.

What happens to old computers?

Old computers are difficult to sell because they are too slow and do not have enough memory to use the latest software. However, there are organizations that take old computers and **refurbish** them. They erase the hard drive, add more memory, and put in faster processors. Then the computers can be used for jobs where the most powerful computers are not necessary, such as word processing. Some refurbished computers are donated to people who cannot afford new machines.

This is a computer class in Zimbabwe. The children are using refurbished computers that were donated.

What other machines can we recycle?

Refrigerators, washing machines, dishwashers, and stoves take up lots of space in **landfills**. But they can be broken up and their parts recycled. Many car parts can also be recycled. Motor oil and batteries can be recycled. Tires can be reused to make crash barriers, chopped up to make soft playground surfaces, and even cut up to make soles for shoes. Modern cars are designed so that many parts are easy to remove for recycling after the car is worn out.

Taking Action: Collect for Nonprofit Organizations

Nonprofit organizations often collect old cell phones and computer printer cartridges, which they recycle to raise money. Ask a parent or teacher to help you find out which organizations raise money this way. Then, organize a cell phone and ink-cartridge drive at your school. Make a collection box and a poster to advertise your drive. Donate what you collect to the nonprofit.

This is a recycling bank in Britain which collects printer cartridges and cell (mobile) phones.

PLEASE

Thank you

NO LOOSE OR RECYCLED
CARTRIDGES
**Computer
Printer Cartridge
Recycling
Bank**
ALL CARTRIDGES
MUST BE IN
ORIGINAL PACKAGING
WITH ALL ITEMS
ORIGINALLY SUPPLIED
**ALSO WANTED
MOBILE PHONES**

WANTED
ORIGINAL
LASER
BUBBLEJET
INKJET
FAX
CARTRIDGES
&
MOBILE
PHONES

Ⓧ **Oxfam**
Registered charity no 202918.

fact file

- In a year, the 60 million inhabitants of Britain produce about 500 million tons of waste. This would fill a line of trucks that would stretch five times around the world.
- Each year, we produce about three percent more waste than the year before. If we take no action, the amount of waste we make will double by the year 2020.
- Each American citizen creates 4.5 pounds (2 kilograms) of **household waste** every day. Together, Americans produce about 210 million tons of household waste.
- Each year Americans throw away enough cardboard to fill 5,000 Olympic-sized swimming pools.
- Seven out of every ten newspapers are recycled in Australia.
- Every year a typical household in Britain throws away:
  - 500 glass bottles and jars
  - 1,000 food and drink cans
  - 400 plastic bags
  - Ten truckloads of green waste
  - Six trees worth of paper
- About 80 million cans go into **landfills** in Britain every day.
- About eight million **disposable** diapers are thrown away in Britain every day.
- Americans throw away 2.5 million plastic bottles every hour!
- Recycling an aluminum can saves enough electricity to run a computer for three hours.

further Reading

Harlow, Rosie, and Sally Morgan. *Garbage and Recycling*. Boston: Kingfisher Books, 2002.

Leeper, Angela. *Landfill*. Chicago: Heinemann Library, 2004.

Woods Samuel G., and Gale Zucker. *Recycled Paper: From Start to Finish*. San Diego, Calif.: Blackbirch Press, 2000.

Glossary

bacteria tiny living things that live in air, water, or soil

compost material that helps plants grow, which is made from the remains of rotting plants

developed describes a country that has advanced industries and where most people have an education, jobs, a place to live, and food to eat

disposable something that is designed to be thrown away after being used

environment our surroundings, including plants and animals, the land, water, and atmosphere, and buildings

extract remove from something

fiber very thin piece of something

fossil fuel fuel that is formed from the remains of plants and animals that died millions of years ago. Fossil fuels include coal, natural gas, and oil (petroleum).

fungi lifeforms such as mushrooms and molds. They are neither plants nor animals.

household waste waste that is made by the people who live in a home

landfill place where waste is buried in deep holes in the ground

methane gas given off by rotting plants

microorganism plant or animal that is too small to see with the naked eye

natural resource useful material that we get from our natural surroundings, such as wood, coal, and rocks

optician person who tests people's sight and figures out what strength of eyeglasses they need

packaging material used to wrap up things you buy, such as plastic bags and cardboard boxes

pollution something that makes air, water, or other parts of Earth's environment dirty

raw material material we get from the Earth in its natural state, which we can then use to make other things

rechargeable battery battery that can be used again and again by putting electricity back into it when it has run out

refurbish repair and add new parts to an old machine so that it can be used again

rot break down into simple chemicals naturally

waste transfer station place where people can take their waste to be recycled or taken to landfill sites

Index